Blessings Beyond Belief

I Am: We Are

Cheryl Lunar Wind and Friends

Blessings Beyond Belief

I Am: We Are

Some of the poems in this collection first appeared in Know Your Way, We Are One, Follow the White Rabbit and Step Into New Earth chapbooks and on facebook.

Cover photo credit to Gibran Larbi, 2025
Front cover design credit to Catherine Preus, 2025

First edition.

Published by Alexander Agency Books,
Mount Shasta, California 96067

ISBN 979-8-9988971-0-8

Blessings
Beyond
Belief

I Am: We Are

Dedicated to my 'love children'
Tim and Jennifer Hershelman.

Preface

The way to *'Blessings Beyond Belief'* is by each of us following our own 'Imperfect Path'.

There may be brutal realizations along the path, but don't allow them to de-rail you. To use a childhood metaphor, be like the little train that kept chugging along to her destination. Only, don't just think you can. Know you can---Own it!

On your journey, practice unilateral acceptance and step into your I Am presence---
Move through doubt and difficulty.
Become the Great We Are and receive *'Blessings Beyond Belief'*.

The Imperfect Path

Life is a contrast of Light and Darkness, Beauty and Pain. Most people seem to want to avoid the darkness and pain not realizing that it is necessary to find oneself in balance you have to walk through darkness. The Imperfect path is about how we weave through both light and dark and even when we take the darker path (the imperfect path) we all make it to our destination. ---Jennifer Hershelman

"You have to look deeper,
way below the anger,
the hurt, the hate,
the jealousy, the self-pity,
way down deeper where the dreams lie.
Find your dream.
It's the pursuit of the dream that heals you."
--Lakota Prayer

Contents

Sacred Pause
by Rune Darling

The World Is Not Falling Apart
It Is Falling Into Place
.

This Is Not The End My Friend
It Is A Sacred Pause
Between What Has Been
And What Is Yet To Come
.

You And I Did Not Arrive
To Battle The Dying World
We Came To Stand Guard
Upholding Sacred Frequencies
.

Heart Work Through
Intuition Is Our Way
We Are Not Too Late
We Are Perfectly On Time
.

BEYOND THE VEIL
by Kazi Ayaz Mahesar

' I '
Beyond that me and mine

' You '
Beyond that you and yours

' We '
Beyond that us and ours

There is this Universe,
That possesses nothing

And nothing possesses it

Our eyes
Do not belong to us

Our visions
Are not our visions

The stardust
Belongs to stars

It has no entity of its own
It has purpose bigger than now

This little lantern
Shines as bright as stars

This little warmth
Is enough to pass a winter

This cube of ice
Can soothe the heart of summer

This parched drought
Can be a harbinger of rain

This little tree
Will age for generations

2

It is beyond
That is me, that is you

It will outlive us
It will leave us behind

Until we know
To live in our shadows

To live in our light
To live it all

Until we are given...
Another chance!

You Have Other Streams
by Kazi Ayaz Mahesar

And mine are with you
You that hide
And I find you

You, and you think it is I
I your universe
And how you paint me?

Whatever you paint
It is You, it is I

A wing when I fall
Wingless when I fly

A ding in your soul
A soul in my heart

I Am : We Are
by Cheryl

When you step into your I Am--
you become the great We Are.

It is the great return.
Who else feels it?

It is glorious to live
connected and free---
like the plants and animals,
just doing their thing
not worrying; all in harmony,
naturally,
Not--
Underdressed, Overdressed
Open, Closed----Fitting in?
Wondering...
Do I belong--
SQueezing ourselves into boxes---
Shrinking down so as to please---

Wanting to be a part,
of something, anything--
Not realizing
We Are the Great I Am.

We Stand Out. No longer
able to hide.
We are tall. Towering. Like Tor.*
This is our tower moment.

We will not go quietly. Not silenced--
any more.

We Are.

*Glastonbury Tor

The Holy Container
by Shivrael

I AM a deep vessel of receiving
of what is poured into me from the Universe
as the Universe.

I AM a holy container of human
just as you are-
experiencing everything through this One consciousness
yet broken into fractals.

We have forgotten how we fit together
but we are remembering in every Now moment.

We are piecing together the grand puzzle of our Oneness
represented by iridescent rainbow crystalline shards
of pure remembrance and knowing.

When we find where we fit with one another;
we mend the greater One into wholeness,

We fuse our memory, our knowing, our power,
and our collective wisdom;
the quantum field ignites with the ancient ones
adding a dimension of greatness.

Woven in are sacred golden threads from the angels-
they hold the mesh of our beingness together in coherence.

We are them and they are we.

Each time that we remember "as above so below"
with the memory of the One that we are,
we create heaven on Earth.

It happens with every breath of
our holy body vessel and
every beat of our heart
simply being in pure presence.

5

Fissures In the Sky
by Kazi Ayaz Mahesar

I will not be seen walking

Through your tears;

Through your laughters,

I will be walking in silence

Not away, but towards...

Towards the reasons

You cry, you laugh

Towards the seasons

Of your sorrow,

Of your joy;

Towards the rainbows

Through your eyes

Towards the heaven

Through your heart,

To whisper the silence

To silence the whisper

To stay the moment

A moment to stay,

To witness, to remember;

The dark night of human soul

The bright light of its dawn,

To witness, to know

How quick it changes

How long it stays,

How near it feels

How far it has to go...

I will be walking...

In this mystery

Of its own journeying,

Of its own witnessing,

Into the oblivions

Of its own fissures...

Into the mirrors

Of its own fusions.

So Speak Up
by Dan Crusey

You might hear somebody saying
"Your choice of words is so so critical "
And you might think to yourself
"I am not articulate enough to speak "
Then you will not speak,
And you will not be heard
But I tell you, it is not so important
How a thing is said
As what is being said
And it is not for any of us
To speak perfectly, because we don't
But it is for all of us
To listen with a will to understand
And I guarantee you
That you have something to say
That somebody needs to hear
So speak up
And be heard

You Have the Power
by Dave Harvey

The power of words, the power of form, the power of emotion,
the power of love, the power of control, the power of fear,
the power of hope, the power of despair, the power of adventure,
the power of slavery, the power of peace, the power of pain,
the power of sight, the power of blindness, the power of hunger,
the power of control, the power of bliss, the power of release,
the power of touch, the power of solitude, the power to hear,
the power to cry, the power to laugh.

Just a few reasons you are here.

I Am Not
by Cheryl

Don't be a dick(tator)--
Always what you want--

Does that work for you?
Not for me--
anymore.

I am not your--
Fill-in
Second choice
or Stand by

I am not your gypsy--
I fly with the fairies.

I am not who I was--
I'm coming up--
No one can stop me.

Men who think life
is a giant grocery store--
I am not anyone's produce.

Sports--
"Play the field"

Fishing--
Catch a good one?
She is not yours--
Throw her back.

Return her to the water,
waters of life.

Don't look my way
because I have moved on.

There is One for me--
He will come at the right time.

I have put out the call.

Just Say No
by Cheryl

I'm not counting days or collecting chips--
But,
After generations of alcoholism--
It's time for some awareness.

I'm sounding the alarm.

Drinking a beer is not a good time,
and a romantic dinner does not need wine.

Ever wonder why natural plants are made 'illegal'
while alcohol is mass produced, marketed and pushed on us?

The alcohol industry has caused more harm to humanity
than any other.

Mind altering substances do just that--
alter your mind, dim your awareness, make you dumb.

Just Say No!

Imperfect
by Elizabeth M. Carrillo

IMPERFECT

Why do I lack completeness
Whilst being aware of my God Within

CONNECTEDNESS

Is it my vessel...
Tangible and perceptible physical affliction
Whilst witnessing healing through my very breath

ACTIVATION

Is it my mental capacity...
Predisposed for failure, fear, self-sabotaging
Whilst engaging in cognitive awareness

REPROGRAMMING

Is it my lack of true faith
Or lack of true belief
In what I think i know?

IMPERFECT

Divine Connection
God
Mother
Father
Buddha
Inner child
Christ consciousness
Angels
Spirit guides
Fairies and fawns
Immortals
Enlightened ones

TO EVERY BEING IN THE UNIVERSE

Is it my connection that's staticky
Or barely recognizable
Or non-existent
... yet I feel it!

Is it a subconscious programming
Throughout my ages and ancestry
That block me from accessing
...yet I still find the link!

IMPERFECT

Mentality/Emotionality
Ego
Deserving mentality
Self-criticism
Emotional instability
Demanding mentality
Distorted reality
Blaming mentality
Pessimistic focus on potential failures

Or how about:
Difficulty with anything uncomfortable
Crutch being suppression and avoidance

Is it my overwhelm that persists daily
Or anxiety - daily
Or my non-existence, little mouse
...yet I am a powerful being DAILY!

Is it my role of caretaker to all
neutral (nay neglector) to my self
...yet I create reality
with my thoughts and actions!

IMPERFECT

Challenges and stacked decks
Cycles that I fear
I can never change
Because they involve others to change
... oh what a belief that is

Cycles I'm not brave enough for
To break off from
Abstain or quit
...yet considering past experiences
I have been valiant in effort and commitment

IMPERFECT
ME

Suffering sea...
all alone on this buoyant-as-fuck boat
Alone with my attachments
Suffering sea...
Of life's continuous challenges
And cycles to overcome
Of the deck stacked against me
And the added turmoil of escaping
is haunting me

But is it escape or something else?
You know what I mean
the potential for liberation

IS HOPE

That in that conclave,
My private room on that boat
In the suffering sea,
I can set myself free
That which is locked
Is locked by ME
Can be unlocked by ME!

Unlocked, Unblocked, Untethered

My freedom from suffering
Was always there in me
Imperfectly perfect me
Hopeful again to step on the shores
And breathe

Being Brave
by Jonathan Hopkins

Being brave is having no fear
even when danger is near
away from fear you steer
and it will all become clear

Move obstacles out of the way
and in this power you will stay
feel this freedom for another day
you can clear the skies away from gray

Black Sheep or Unicorn
by Archi Thorne

One families "Black sheep" is another families "Unicorn"....

Exit= the school of duality through the zero point neutral
ous godsource field to find access to your multi-dimensional
expression with a fully open heart, speaking and living
your truth with the "All" "that is One", while tending to
and caring for our Great Mother while walking in harmonic
balance with your Divine Masculine and Feminine aspects in
unity, allowing your Monad to be driven by your Over-soul
and attracting others mirroring your experience in a
way that equally gives and receives healing.....

Superhuman to Enlightened Being of Light
by Zarah Chelsie Nicole Wolivar

I am creative.

My frequencies must merge with others that have loving
frequencies to support me.
If I am forced to be in lower frequencies then I will use
my free will to find those in higher vibration.
My consciousness is not allowed to be punished or judged.
I am Unlimited Consciousness!

I have the right to transform my body with my consciousness.
Can I change my DNA cells and evolve into a Superhuman?
Yes I can!

Ignore what the scientists say about your DNA cells evolving.
It is what I say that matters.
Can I go from a Superhuman to an Enlightened Being of Light?
Yes I can! No one can tell me otherwise!
I choose where my soul goes and not what the false god tells me.
I do not accept false gods or false angels that limit my free will or
power.
You are messing with the wrong woman.
I accept myself. I am that fire of light. I am the transformation into
a crystalline being of light.

I AM
Unlimited,
Blessings,
Consciousness,
Supportive,
Empowered,
Creative!!!

A Woman that calls herself Pink has Inner Strength
by Cheryl

Be the color you love.

See a pink halo around the sun,
Wings made of clouds.

Roses are forever.

A dragon leads the way.

Drum the beat of your heart.

Light the Fire.

Snowflakes always come.

Pass the sage.

We are all angels.

Pink Sprinkles
by Jennifer Hershelman

I am pink sprinkles

Powerful

Singing rainbows into existence

Celebrating with the chirping doves
as the crows make their way home

I am shimmering honey

Graceful

Dancing with the grandmothers
as we honour the glorious rising of the Sun

I am Golden

Open, Expressing, Becoming

                    Wiggle, Fizz, Rhythm

The Imperfect Path*
by Cheryl Lunar Wind

On Our Brave Mother Earth--
the path is imperfect--
But Spirit's sense of humor
brings unlimited blessings.

Watch out for consciousness traps--
We all have unique experiences--

Blessings in disguise.

**Surrender
like the White Dove of Peace.**

How do we handle our fears?
Become buoyant like Buddha--
Play with your inner child--
Be tolerant of your feelings.
We all have them.
Self-love holds the key.

We Are Unlimited--
Hold your power in balance.
Be understanding.

In the Brave New Earth--
Unicorns hold council & support us.

We time travel to the Void--
where the creativity threshold exists.

Hop in--
No telling
what you will find.

The Void is at the center of
each & everyone's heart space.

Be a Heart Adventurer
on Mother Earth,
anything is possible--

deep canyons
shallow valleys
and mountain highs

It is a journey we must make alone--
but it is not lonely.
We alone choose our path--
and it will be
*Perfectly Imperfect Art.**

*title inspiration from Jennifer Hershelman
*Pradeep Nawarathna

Perfectly Imperfect Art
by Pradeep Nawarathna

Hold your own hand when the path gets tough,
Love yourself first when days feel rough.
Your journey is yours, no need to compare,
Take one small step, breathe in fresh air.
Dreams need tending, like seeds that you sow,
Give yourself time and space to grow.
One life, one heart—perfectly imperfect art,
Be gentle, be patient, love who you are.

Resentment
by Le'Vell Zimmerman

Resentment can be released beloved.

Slowly, but surely.

It has always been about you...

Do you have the capacity of compassion to truly forgive and let go?

Nothing was done "to you"...

Within the hologram it was truly all by you.

For you.

God.

We are expecting you...

11:11

Fun!
by Dave Harvey

As you become aware of something more,
many ideas will present themselves.
Comfort yourself with those that feel best,
those that are most fun.

Do not underestimate fun.

There are a multitude of things to worry about,
fun is not one of them.

-A Pleiadian passing by

Finding Permission
by Cheryl

What were my gifts?

It's not about darkly funny women
with drug problems having sex with strangers...

It was like the hand of God picking
me off the ground.

I, too, am tired of being brave,
Each day since getting sober I've
tried to practice kneeling before
the things that I know I can't control.

It's all about--
What We Are Carrying

And our Willingness
to let it go--

Give Yourself Permission

Samples of Source
by Cheryl

Vibrant, glorious, invading--
Samples of Source
like the fateful
meeting of crab and seagull,
sand covered remains
life squelched
by shouting, streams
of rain--

If they told me,
I would've stayed home that day.

Paradise Can't Happen Without You
by Shivrael

I am flying as the falcon that I saw circling near the river
As I sat on the bank and watched her, spirit's messenger.
I am now choosing to follow the wind currents upward
upward to a higher level,
a higher dimension,
a higher perspective.

Looking down, I see the sacred silver river
with a shiny surface and strong rapids
like a silver thread stretching through green.

This is our timeline, the future one is here now.
The water is the thread of silver that flows-
representing the Golden Age.
We are here, finally, we really are in that river.
The Golden Age is here now.
We are on that timeline collectively.
Nothing and no one can stop it-
because the flow is so strong now,
from the momentum of choice-
The people have chosen a new reality based on love.
The flow is so strong now
because of all the angels who have given us wings.
The flow is so strong now
because the galactic beings
Help us remember who we are
and what we came for.

My higher self tells me about our Oversoul,
represented by our beloved soul family
that we recognize with the feeling of home
felt in our hearts upon
meeting and being with them.
My soul recognizes your soul
from the deepest part of my being
and takes a bow,
Grateful for this connection
so divinely guided.

"What is our Oversoul's purpose?"

26

I ask this of my higher self, and receive the answer.
We are here as architects of the New Earth.
An architect is a visionary.
We are the ones envisioning and bringing the new way of being
as the Golden Age births.
We get to be the pioneers and create from what we imagine
as to what the Earth is calling for; How exciting!

We already have the keys and codes.
We already have the visions.
In meeting one another, we are sharing,
telling one another the future reality that we imagine
from our mind's eye and our hearts
to one another.
This listening, sharing, and telling of what we imagine
anchors in what we came here for,
It's the same as what we wish to create and co-create
to uplift Earth, to renew the elements,
Earth, air, fire, and water.
We bring love and care,
creativity, healing and most of all freedom
to the humans and other beings.
When we share, we are anchoring the New Earth
We are allowing our sacred blueprints within
coded in our DNA
to come forth and come together with others
The highest divine plan is coming to fruition
in synergy, synchronicity, and divine unity
and in service to the One we are.

You may think that you are small
And that what you know doesn't matter
But God put it there.
It is oh so important because your heart
came with dreams and plans
to turn this reality into paradise.

Little one, speak your truth
dream your dreams,
envision and share them,
Speak them, and take steps toward them
because paradise can't happen without you.

Into The Lion's Den
by Vivian Marie McIntosh

When you're observing life from a higher
perspective than those around you
One might feel like Daniel being cast into the den
where lions skeptically surround you

Remember Not 2 4get, to have no fear regardless
of who or what you might face
Pronoia, Providence, and Prophecy paved the path
which led you to this place

Choose to have faith in your creator and trust
in your own heart
The Threefold flame is where God left his signature,
a Divine Spark

Nobody else outside of that can say what was
written on yours
Like Moana and Maui earned theirs, we receive our
own fish hooks and oars

Our very own conduits, though they can not be
held or seen
These spiritual tools are our reward for activating
demigod DNA inside...if yanno what Eye mean!

Everyone's gift will be beautiful and unique,
different from everyone else
Though we are ALL one, we each came to leave
our own print and escape from our own hells

Only after we allow our ego to die, can our soul
then become resurrected
Our higher self can take the lead and through
storms and chaos our inner child be directed

So as Eye continue onward and upward
Stacking up jars of healing herbs in my cupboard

Eye don't really mind what others think of me
Knowing they aren't able to yet see what Eye see

Loving myself and happy to see beyond the veil
Mastering myself with no worry if Eye fall or fail

Trusting in my own Heart Power and knowing that the master
fails more times than the beginner ever even attempts
No time to say Hello, Goodbye to those who can't see me,
too busy connecting dots, collecting puzzle pieces and
making it make sense

Like Alice, Eye too have visited Wonderland after
falling down the deep rabbit hole of Truth
The things Eye found and experienced there
changed me forever, giving me now, extensively deep roots

It's true what Carl Jung said about trees and what
they need to do to be able to grow up into heaven
Everyone is so busy moving around without even
putting their bare feet on the ground, totally missing the lesson

Our names are ALL-ready written in The Book of Life,
yet in order to graduate from 3D Earth games and
join the New Golden Age
It's imperative while we're taking these individual Soul Tests
which directly influence the collective, so be sure to turn over the
page!!!

If you're only focused on good deeds to get
your name in the book
It's over your own demons and shadow
that you'll just happen to over look

To earn your cap, gown and Divinity Diploma
And to God, you yourself be a Sweet Aroma

Conquer yourself, as to not project your inner turmoil out
Learn to maintain your own frequency no matter what,
as well as have faith even when in doubt

If you ALL-ways take the high ground and use heart power
In addition to standing solid in your brilliant light,
you also learn to glow in your darkest hour

Out of the Tunnel
by Rene Moraida

When I stepped out of the light tunnel and into the realm of Mother
Earth, I did not know the vast array of earthly powers that claim to
rule here.

Kings and queens, in their royal courts.
Popes, chosen by cardinals in conclaves,
Petty politicians, delusional dictators, tempestuous tyrants,
Cunning charlatans, tricksters and thieves, murderers and
monsters.
There is a sickening madness that envelopes and consumes them.

What happened here? Did they forget they where they came from?
Where did their light go--what spell was cast to corrupt and harden
their hearts?

It is written that the elves woke up the trees.
They are guardians here to help us navigate this plane of existence.
Helping us to breathe and connect and heal.
The plants and flowers opened my mind and heart,
And the great white dove of peace opened my crown
and flooded my chakras with the amrita from heaven.

I have to block out the darkness to find my light.
I am finding my Buddha within.
I am guided by radiant and brave unicorns.
My ancestors and the angelic realm stand with me.
I sound my golden angel trumpet not to warn of the Armageddon,
But to beseech the free peoples of Gaia to wake up!
Face your fears! Be unafraid!
Tap into your unlimited power!

Go now to the golden libraries of remembrance.
Through your discovery you will awaken.
You can outmaneuver the maze of consciousness traps that will
seek to Ensnare you and lead you off your path.

30

You are an energy master, a light warrior,
a beacon for those who have forgotten.
You are the calm and the chaos, the yin and the yang.
You bring the destruction and the regeneration.

So I call you now to remember why you came here.
I call you to walk your imperfect path.
It will be made perfect by your energy field that ripples out
To disrupt the matrix and transmute any and all discord.

Walk the imperfect path,
for the day break of a new world is upon us.
It is not yet time to return home, the Source needs you here.
You are on a mission, you child of the holy grail.
Lucid light, it is time to shine!

Dandelions and Sunflowers*
by Jennifer Hershelman

Blessings child, we are with you,
You have been very brave
Overcoming
Becoming
Transforming
                        the fears you've faced
            into Gentle Strength

The white dove of Peace
flies with the healing winds
you have helped to put into place.

Mother Earth is anew & abounds
with unlimited creativity & opportunities
to move forward.

We have passed the Threshold--
the times of old have been laid to rest.

It is up to you to see it through.

What kind of world do you want to create?

The birds sing of patience,
as the winds bring healing and gentle guidance,
the waters murmur to themselves of all the great surprises,
the earth, the dirt and the trees hold us steady
as the chaos of change winds down.

The unicorns release bubbles of inspiration
for those still feeling stuck.

Watch out for the gnomes,
for though they are great guides and builders of/for our new paths,
they are mischievous with a very big sense of humor.

The crows stand watch keeping our energies protected,
none shall pass--
any whom try to keep us from our path.

The leaders are being reminded who really rules the land.

So listen to the forest.
Embrace your inner child
& Go dance, sing and play!

Create the new world this DAY.

*title inspiration from Zarah Nicole Wolivar

Family
by Cheryl

I am having a talk with the little girl---
Hiding inside me. I am telling her it is all right.
She is safe now.
I will protect her--
She remembers her dad's hands around her throat one morning
before she got out of bed---
saying "Why'd you have to come and ruin everything?".

Mom dropping her/me off with a bag of clothes.
Why was she always trying to get rid of me?

We were always moving. No stable ground.
No friends, family or anchor to hold on to.

The dog of choice was a boxer--we always had one or two around.
My favorite was a white female named Lucille.
Somehow she got sick, and my parents refused to pay the vet--
I tried with my waitress tips---
piles of change pouring on the floor as I slipped at work.
My first 'real' boyfriend was my manager at Western Sizzlin
Steakhouse, spending evenings and free time, cozying watching
Excalibur.
He got fired for drinking on the job, and left without even saying
good bye.

I grew up in Opelika Alabama.
When I went out I was the only white girl in the bar---
I wasn't afraid---
They treated me better than my family did.

My uncle that took me sled riding tried to have sex with me.
I adored him.
(My family's frequent moving saved me from that mishap)

When I talked about the comments and sexual passes my stepdad
made---my family called me Liar and labled me Mentally ill.
Them.
Their problem---It is a repeating problem---like a record, at the end,
going round and round, never stopping.
Lies. Shame. Blame.

So, this is family; no wonder I feel safer alone.
What lesson did I ask for this lifetime?
Self-love and Strength of Soul.

(I put this healing off for as long as I could)
It's time now.

Farm Living
by Cheryl

The joys of living on the farm--
(sparkling white) ground covering
glitters like wedding cake frosting--

the wheat poking up, thru
in places--
around the wooden fence posts.

A jeep, with a crank starter--
children playing
on snow sleds--

Days long forgotten--
Dogs & kids pulling snow sleds
Farm living at best.

At Open Sky Gallery
by Cheryl

How about an elephant walking a tight rope?

Waterfalls coalescing below a family of pine trees.

Ancestry--remembering those who came before us.

Whales blowing and traveling together.
Togetherness.

Bird of Paradise flowers--the Ocean--
my time in Maui.

The intelligent stare from a horse's eye.

When the leaves turn scarlet, gold and green--
Isn't there a saying
"Red, Gold & Green"?

Justice comes in many colors and shapes---
The Native American mother and her papoose,
a Chinese Emperor and a black & white foto
of Martin Luther King.

Then, there's a splash of gold
matching the golden lovebirds--
and yellow centered daisies.

The Little Mermaid
perched on a rock--full of curiosity
holding onto her treasure,
what we'd call garbage.
Bright Sun circle over the horizon.
Her joy, in the new.

The berth of it all--
human creation in the form of architecture--
Water--a medium, a home and
streams of intelligence.

Faces, Flowers and Blank Slates

Dried Potatoes
by Snow Thorner

John's phone rings. It's his sister saying her son, our nephew Matt had a severe car accident. Many broken limbs, shattered pelvis. He hangs up. We are both in shock, crying. So afraid for the pain he must be in.

I flashback to Thanksgiving when Matt and his kids were last here. How upset John and I were about Matt's son, our grand nephew Diego, who thought it was fine to prepare instant boxed potatoes as part of Thanksgiving dinner.

We questioned Matt and his daughter, our grand niece Sophie, asking what they thought of it? As if preparing boxed potatoes for a holiday was the worst crime in the world! They both loved the freeze-dried potatoes. John and I thought they were all nuts.

In a heartbeat, I clearly see what fools we were.
Now Matt's life hangs on a thread and we wasted precious loving energy fussing about d r i e d p o t a t o e s.

Brave New World
by Lilapa

In this Brave New World---

We are overcoming
        Our
collective inner dictator--

With the gentleness of a White Dove and
a sense of humor only spirit could bestow.

Yes,
When we face
our fears together
with fierce discernment--

The blessings pour forth...
Sometimes in disguise,
Sometimes on a fleeting unicorn,
Sometimes in a gushing flood
       of tangible emotion.

We are at a threshold.
Is buoyancy pulling us in,
holding us back or
both...

THE VOID-NOT A VOID-DON'T AVOID
by 'Greenie' Yvonne Trafton

(Warning- this poem may contain swear words)

The Void of Creativity. Blessings! We are brave.
Overcoming Fucking Fear.
Face Your Fears with the White Dove of Peace.
Watch for consciousness traps even if you're
Fucking Afraid. You have unlimited Spirits!
Have a Sense of Humor, they are all Blessings in Disguise!
Follow Spirit's Humor--Be a Time Traveler Of Sobriety of mind,
touch my Buddha Within; with a playful mind and heart.
It's all a unique experience-don't be a dictator. Blame no one.
Surrender to sobriety of consciousness on Threshold Tolerance
of Buoyancy of a Magical Unicorn.
Be brave on the rock. Be gentle power with Discernment, love
Mother Earth. Be playful, be in self-empowerment. Empowerment
is the answer.
Die while alive, die while alive!
"Give death to what does not serve you."
Loose the baggage! Die while alive. Life is Unlimited.
Be a Unicorn one way or another.

The Void, Not a Void, Don't Avoid!
Chase away Avoidance. If you avoid, Life will Bitch Slap You to wake
up. Life's funny like that. Life, an Imperfect Path with you in the
way....(lol) Life--

Not What You Think it is,
Life nothing like I thought it would be when I was young.
Life's hard, Life's a school, at times a school of hard knocks.
Life is not for sissies.
Life's only short because we make it so; we waste most of it, we
waste time;
Time Is Not A Friend, time will rob us at our own expense, don't be
one's own thief;
Be your own Robin Hood,
steal from one's own wasted time, reclaim your time, reclaim self,
thrive, thrive Little Bird Fly, Fly High as a Golden Eagle.
Be one's own Phoenix Rising, Oh Phoenix rise from one's own ashes,
rise from one's own flames, from the fire of waste reclaim one's
own life, rise from the fire. Rise Up!
39

Die While Alive. Destroy what does not serve one's self--
Destroy what does not serve one, Destroy one's baggage.
Be like Shiva the Destroyer, The Creator, The Giver of Life,
Create-A-New.
Rise Well, Rise Well with the Power of Durga and Ganesha!
Stand tall, Rise above thyself. Rise Up, Stand Up,
Die While Alive humans.
Transform, Transmute into one's High-Self. Be your potential.

BE IN BALANCE.

To die while alive is the goal of Humans--the Universe is not done
being created,
Humans are here on Earth to help with "Creation".
If we choose to accept this challenge--
What is a challenge anyway but an obstacle of the mind!
LOOSE THE MIND.

Life is a SPIRAL, We Learn in a SPIRAL, Don't SPIRAL.
Time Travel To Our Future Self.
Don't Avoid! The Void, Not A Void, Don't Avoid. Step into the Void.

Avoidance is a killer, the killer of Higher Self, the killer of Higher
Consciousness.
Also,
Embrace your Shadow Self. We are Yin & Yang, Light & Dark.
Do your Shadow Work! Do Not Avoid your shadow side-there's lots
of "juice" there!

Don't Avoid---Get out of your story. Die while alive.
Rewrite your story. Rewrite your story. Rewrite your story.
REWRITE YOUR OWN AKASHA RECORD----
(The Watchers) are watching!
"The Void-Not A Void-Don't Avoid"
                              AHO!

"The Watchers" are "Star Nation Beings of Light" who are the
writers of EVERYONE'S (Akasha Records). We each through all time
have an Akasha Records Book in the Akasha Library. "The Watchers"
are also--- in charge of the Akasha Library. We can always look at
our own Akasha Record Book.

Spiral
by Danielle Divinity

Spiral out,
Release all negative patterns and doubt,
Re-write what your life is about
Break the chains of repetition
and redefine the human condition
because here's a forlorn premonition
for those with a close-minded disposition:
If you don't tap into your intuition,
You'll become the definition of demolition--
Geometry codes gone haywire
The situation is growing dire
The evil ones conspire
Striking at heels like a viper
They are this generation's vampire
Soon to be cast into great lakes of fire
Son of Atom, stretch forth your wings
Open your third eye; see the condition of things
Break loose from the binding of Saturn's rings
For you are the child of gods and kings!

-DMB is We

Path to Heaven
by Daniel Stone

Moving softly through
A conflict zone
Invisible rose
Avoiding bombs
And smell the
Runic
Path to Heaven

White Dove of Peace
by Shima Moore

Unlimited I am
Filled with Blessings
Gentle power rising to the surface

Mother Earth ignites creativity and wisdom
Self-love overcomes all impinging fear

The inner child now brave and sovereign,
Courage empowers her to cross the threshold of consciousness
traps
Blessings in disguise,
these unique and necessary experiences,
give birth to the Medicine Buddha within

Penetrating illusion and confusion in the Void,
She emerges, surrendered,
a White Dove of Peace.

Winners
by Cheryl

the wheels
go Round and Round...

This journey
is not a race
But a Marathon.

We are the winners!

If you are still here,
walking and talking
on Earth now----

You are a Winner.

Keep on keeping on.

Being
from Dave Harvey

This journey has no destination,
it's really not a journey, it's just being.

When you begin to live through your heart the race dissolves,
belief structures crumble.
This is not without its challenges.
You would have it no other way.
Embrace where you are, complain less.
Give yourself a break.
Extend that courtesy to all.
-Nuri

LIRA NATION
by Lira Rene Christian

Boomerang swing with a cosmic decree
33, 3, 3, 3, countin' down with heat
Real ones comin' home, time to fix the breach
When the veil gets torn, that's when truth gon' speak
You don't touch our babies, don't cross our queens
Now the fire awakens in the in-between
They twisted the code, now I'm here to clean
Got five days left, then I crash the scene

Where my God's artifacts? Bring 'em back intact
They missed the fountain at midnight, now feel the crack
Pay the price in full, no duckin' that
Every stolen gem, every sacred pact
I want my toys, my wheels, my throne
They thought I'd forget? Nah, I'm carved in stone
This a Lira decree from a hidden zone
And the debts ain't erased till the gold's all shown

Royalty in Portugal, count the lines
Read the blood, it's etched in design
Sir Wallace spirit in my spine
Medal of Honor, both sides divine
We the oldest bank, the first elite
Truth locked down till it cracked concrete
You don't steal from us and leave discreet
We the Liras, baby, now rise and repeat

Peek-a-boo, peek-a-boo, truth revealed
We back from the shadow with a sword to wield
Ancestors chantin', the seals unsealed
And the wicked gon' feel what justice feels
Lira Nation, crown in hand
We don't beg, we just command
From stars to stone, we take our stand
Bloodline gold, God's chosen brand

The Dragons Return
by Lira Rene Christian

I saw the altar crack in flame
The dragons rose and called my name
Levethian stirred the ocean floor
His eyes like storms, his mouth a roar

Nocthyris blazed across the sky
Burned the truth in every lie
He haunts your sleep, he sears your breath
He is the fire, the light, the death

Auranox tore the heavens wide
No chariot left a place to hide
Winds obey his silent call
He breaks the pride before the fall

Terranox rose from molten core
Split the land from shore to shore
His voice shook roots and toppled towers
He is the quake in final hours

Thamuraz stood on mountain high
A flame beneath a judgment sky
He guards the peaks you stole in vain
And marks your blood with holy flame

The Etheridge Realm begins to turn
Its gates ignite, its scrolls burn
The book of Amos now alive
You had your chance, you won't survive

For every cave and ocean deep
The dragons fly, the dragons keep
There is no place, no stone, no sky
Where you can flee and not reply

The Lord has spoken, sealed with breath
Your hiding place becomes your death
Return what's mine, or face the tide
There is no time, there's nowhere to hide
— Merlin, the Master of Dragons by Birthright

Calling Power and Cord Cutting
by Ulrikke Aagaard

I call my power back to me, from every person, place, entity
From every space, portal, time and dimension
From every connection, attachment and vessel where I left it

Anyone and anything that is attempting to siphon my energy
You DO NOT have my consent to use my vitality--
I call my power back
I now release that which is not my own

I lay down the weight that doesn't belong to me,
as well as the weight that does
I forgive all things, all people and all others. I forgive myself.

I cloak myself in a bright light of protection - Impenetrable
I shed light to my shadows and lovingly work through all
insecurities,
flaws and self-destructive habits.
I honor those parts of myself and I love them to life
Any and every soul tie is now disconnected.
My mind is decluttered, and eye see clearly--
Those who no longer serve me, and the mindsets attached to them

I take time for self-evaluation to uncover what in me connected me.
I heal my broken places.
I take up space in my own life;
I unapologetically do the same in the rooms that I walk into--
My light, my energy speaks for me before I ever open my mouth,
My vibration reverberates and pushes away any energy
that's not mine,
And I Align.
Knowing that this is all that is required of me.

I receive my Power Back.

The Returning
by Cheryl

the same words, different
arrangements---
over and over and over again.

This year will be different--
I will ride that bike I bought,
goto a festival, and quit worrying so much.

I will return to myself.

Seagulls of All Time
by Kazi Ayaz Mahesar

Seasons of Seeing
Seasons of Flying

Far away yet not far
A Sea in between

A Hill, A Glacier
A Tree in between

Same Land, Same Sky
Where We May Hide

Where We May Not See!
Where We May Not Hear!

No more blinded by a Blindfold
No more hidden by a Veil

This Light
This Season of Seeing

Seasons of Heart
Seasons of God Within

Seasons of Lamps
Seasons of Stars

No Woods of Wildfire
No guns, no gunshots

No to all evils
No to all cruelty

Peace is made with Peace
War is of the Devil

Sadly, and more so
War is of the people

Still in the days of past
Still in the caves of past

Nothing creates hunger
As much as the greed

Might is Weak
Rights are for All Life

Be Gentle
Violence creates Violence

Let It
Suffer as it caused to suffer

Justice in men, in women
Justice be upheld

There are gardens that are burnt
There Are Gardens to Regrow

A flower takes a season
A tree takes years

And this time
Is only a fraction of a moment

Aim what you are tasked
Deconstruct illusions

It is Beginning Again
It is Beginning in Now

Like the Rivers of All Colour
Like the Seagulls of All Time

Double Date
by Cheryl

Double take--
take to make

spin a yarn
tell a tale--fib
just a little white lie
(make an impression)

Double dip
Double meaning

Chinese checkers--rolling, running away
Chinese fire drill---
In and Out

Double dutch
skip along

Double date--
double trouble

Double take--
Do it again.

Name that Tune
by Cheryl

Up, down,
Clown around

Here, there, where?

Cause--
cause & effect.

Why?

Because.

Love fiercely--
go gently into the nite.

Winning, Loosing--

Calling, Stalling--

Naming, Gaming

Play the Game of Life!

It's 642, Who are you!?!
by Vivian Marie McIntosh

Eye'm Mad As A Hatter
Or A Phrygian Genius
Dropping Some Orenda
Dance In A Rose Like Venus

Looped In My Own Cycle
So Many Times It's Broken
Creative And Conservative
Careful Of Words Spoken

Daughter Of The Most High
Cosmic Mother Turned Milliner
Rebirthing Myself As Needed
While Transmuting The Sinister

Mastering ALL The Elements
An Avatar, The Last Airbender
Purifying My Aura To Be Full Of Light
Reflecting Low Vibes Back To Sender

Guided By Love Of My Own Warrior Heart
Under Divine Rule An Authoritive Protection
Halo On Straight, Wings Ready And Waiting
To Fly Me Above Any Dimming Projection

Balancing And Grounding Electrical Energy
Seeking ALL Hidden Truth With Ancient Eyes
ALL Things The Masses Close Their Minds To
Everything Taught To Be Feared And Despised

Reject What Shows Up To Lower My Frequency
Keep My 2 Cents To Myself, Not Paying Attention
Fighting That Nonsense Isn't What Eye Came For
Here On Earth To Complete An Ancestral Mission

Wearing The Full Armor Of God Which Eye Earned
A Cowardly Lioness Could Not Wield This Sword
Gift For Speaking Truth When My Voice Was Shaking
Became So Brave And Bold Eye Can't Be Ignored

Holding My Shield Built With Faith Of Steel
Breastplate Of Righteousness On My Chest
Protecting A Heart Of Gold Full Of Lotsa Love
Knowing What's Yet To Come Is Truly Best

Nelipot Feet Covered In Dirt And Shod In Peace
Covering My Crown With A Helmet Of Salvation
Remembering Not To Ever Forget To Put On My Cap
Indicates Freedom And Liberty From The Plantation

Eye Enjoy Weaving Magic With The Written Word
A Straight Up Sacred Poetic Priestess Logophile
Speaking Up For The Innocent That Have No Voice
Helping To Hunt The Hunters And The Pedophile

Some People Are Unaware Of The War We're In
Just Like The Cartoon Residents Of Ba Sing Se
Lucky For Them, A Group Of Like Hearted Masters
Wearing White Hats Are Here Freeing Out Our Way

The Color Represents A Celestial Virtue
No Relevance With Our Skin Or Racism
Nothing Can Stop What They Have Started
Revolution And Renaissance Of Humanism

Free Will Is The Only Thing Keeping Us Slaves
In Programmed Boxes We Been Surviving In
Step Up Outta Those Four Walls Of Patriarchy
Embrace And Embody The New Age Feminine

Grim Peanut Butter
by Lira Rene Christian

It's not easy being God's Grim Reaper
Bearing light where the night grows deeper
They smile wide with their hands outstretched
But behind the veil, there's a knife in the flesh

I come in peace with a flame in hand
They see the glow, they don't understand
They chase the gold, they curse the dove
They choose the greed, forget the love

They build their thrones on shifting sand
But I was carved by the Father's hand
I walk through fire, untouched by hate
Because I carry a heaven-made fate

Take away fear, the false crowned king
And hear the sound of freedom ring
No more chains, no more disguise
Just open hearts and open skies

You gave me words that shake the ground
Verses born where truth is found
They tried to trade my soul for gain
But I rose like thunder through the rain

Love is unity, love is breath
It conquers time, it laughs at death
And business blooms where peace has grown
When every heart feels not alone

So let them talk and play their game
I bear the fire, I speak Your name
The Reaper's robe, now white as snow
I came to reap, so life can grow

And in the stillness, bold and true
I spread the word like morning dew
I break the curse, I break the rule
And yeah—I love peanut butter too.

Jah's Mountain
by Lira Rene Christian

Oh theory, theory, theory,
Leader of the ones who scheme,
Tried to cast my blood away,
But the mountain knows its dream.

Spit out what don't belong,
Keep the roots deep in the ground,
As the light begins to shine,
Your false ways come tumbling down.

Poison brewed in darkened hands,
Served with whispers, laced with lies,
But the truth will cleanse the land,
Watch the storm clear out the skies.

Don't let the door hit you,
As you fade into the sea,
Far from here, your island waits,
Built on greed and blasphemy.

I know those who walk in truth,
They don't sell the faith for gold,
They don't twist the words of love,
For power, lust, or bitter hold.

This is Jah's mountain, not your throne,
Not a place for games and chains,
Stone by stone, we'll tear it down,
Raise it up with love again.

Free the people, clear the air,
Let the echoes fade away,
What was hidden now revealed,
Let the righteous lead the way.

Brothers and Sisters:
by Cheryl

Mama Shasta is calling her family home---
like a mother hen gathering her chicks.

Do you hear the call?

I walk the path--
that Saint Germaine has laid out,
the original pied-piper with a magic flute.

The tune is true beauty,
Enticing, Circling, Protecting
Holding us with arms of love.

I Am by Cheryl

In the cosmos, I am
a Solar Quartz--
shimmering, sparkling.

My blinding starlight
brings healing, love and
synchronicity.

I shine mauve, orange and
lavender-- all at once.

I smell like cinnamon and
sassafras tea.

I run like a black equine---
Secretariat.

I hobnob my way to write
poetry at the cattywampus!

I AM
by Danielle Divinity

Acceptance is divine--
Because we always draw a line between
what is mine and yours but it's fine because...
It's a sign that it's all within the grand design.

We are particles of matter made to matter by non-matter
what is it you're serving on the reality platter?

It's making us fatter, it's making us sadder;
It's time for a ladder to a higher dimension of descension,
Are you even paying attention?

But you are because you are always paying something and
taking to give so you can give to take and
It is what It isn't and It is what It is because It's always been.

All seeing from the singular eye, forgetting to re-member--
It is all eyes seeing and not seeing, blinking in and out of existence
and God, it takes persistence and so much resistance to forget the
distance.

And still,
We drip drop from the paintbrush of God, pretending to be a piece
of artwork frozen in an image imagining imagination in the image of
God. God perceiving God and the perceived lack of God on a stage
called Earth. We are all divine jokers playing a cosmic game of hide
and seek as we watch it leak from our eyes onto our cheek
pretending--
to be meek, to be weak, but also the peak of all that is and was and
ever will be.

We are but the symphony experiencing itself as a single note,
A beach experiencing itself as a grain of sand,
An ocean experiencing itself as a drop.

A divine dichotomy expressing duality,
To be or not to be is the question and the answer
happening together but separately.

60

Do you see what I mean, when I say I lucid dream--
Not everything is as it may seem, because I am
the Conciousness-Stream choosing what I wish to perceive--
currently I wish to deceive but I want you to to know
I still believe in Me, We, the One in all and All in None.

We are the begotten son behold the weight of a ton and say it is
done because there's nowhere else to run and it's no longer fun
to forget to remember--
to be limited and lacking like the mindless fracking of the soul and
still we are tracking but clacking like empty bones wasted on a
frame covered in skin thinking we can sin...

But love will always win.

-DMB is We

Teddy's Easter Transmission:
from Sabina and Herd of Light

The tendency is to
cave in your heart.
Yes, there is a season to cave in,
and perhaps to seal or even barricade the threshold.
But don't get stuck there.
Don't get tripped up by the illusion of the conviction
that the boulder blocking the door is impossible to move.

The Center
even the center of a boulder,
even a strategically, intentionally placed boulder -
yes, its center too,
is Luminous Emptiness.

And when the True Nature of this boulder reveals itself,
then it easily transforms.
Then the corpse hidden in the cave, hidden from view,
reveals its True Nature
as a Body of Light.

The True Nature
of HUman heart
under pressure
is Supernova -

just like coal's nature
under pressure
is Diamond.

The New Earth,
The Resurrection Body,
The Diamond Body,
The Supernova Heart
has risen

Here
Now.
It is time to feel the
Diamond Body
that you are,

62

The Diamond Body
that is all of Nature,
The Diamond Body that is
The New Earth,
The Cosmos of you,
and of me
as One.

Today is the day
to silently proclaim
the Good News
in and out
the blow hole of
your Supernova Heart!

- with endless Easter Love,
 Teddy, Sabina & Herd of Light

School House Earth
by Shivrael

Blessed we are
to surrender our shadows
for we have walked
in the valley of being triggered.

Everyone is fighting an inner battle
to embrace self-love
when they are fucking afraid.
Let this be a reminder
to be kind to everyone.
You don't know
what they are facing.

Sometimes, speaking out
and having a voice takes courage.
We want to be authentic
yet navigating conflict
makes it difficult.

With gentle power
I witness "the troublemaker within"
who wants to sabotage
the flow state I'm in
with overthinking and
getting stuck in consciousness traps.

I take these vows:
I'll walk into my shadows
and turn them over to see them clearly
from every angle.

I will surrender to discovering
my own shortcomings
with vulnerability.

I know there is some purpose here
in overcoming struggle.
Earth life brings us to our knees
with the challenges of simply existing.
Even so, life has blessings to offer
so that we can realize Heaven on Earth-
Right here, right now, in this holy moment.

Open Hearted Curiosity
by Le'Vell Zimmerman

Consider a dimension where all that you have created here doesn't exist beloved...

Indeed, a much dimmer experience to say the least...

Just know that the "shadow self" is still struggling with this kind of disappointment you are presently healing from, where now is the place where you can continue expanding upon and sharing the beauty you naturally demonstrate via your authenticity in being a true gift to this world.

Disappointment comes from the Ego Mind identities expectations, where the mind identities purpose serves us naturally via our "perspective driven curiosity" until there is deeper awareness, trust, and connection with The Higher Self's refined and much more loving intentions at the core of our Being.

Your open hearted curiosity is allowing "your gifts and secrets" to surface.

To trust yourself is to trust God.

-ArchAngel Michael

Treasure Hunt **by Cheryl**

Do you have a broken heart?

Rescue the shards of your heart.
They are treasure.

Search and Rescue.

What is hiding
down
In the
basement of your heart?

Go inward--
to the ward of your heart.

Go deep--dive
to the depths
of your soul.

Dive for treasure.
Treasure Hunt.

Go deep
into the
abyss of nothing.

Enter the Void--

The Black Hole
of complete emptiness.

Only then,
      can you
Run
with your wild horses.

Creative Captains
by Mercy Talley

We are here to
Claim Our Positions
as Creative Captains of
Our Own Sovereign Ships
So to Sail out of Sewers
into Sun Shining Truth ~

I Am Winged & Ready
How About You...

Let's Go Team Humanity ~
Use Our Diversity
to Strengthen & Unify

I Have Arrived
by A'Marie B. Thomas-Brown

Arriving in this place where
all the unanswered questions
and contextual thesis
converge in this sea of unknown
to be seated within the framework
of remembrance.

To pre-exist in the realm of
brainless minds and bloodless hearts
to pulsate amid the jargon
of a world that
though having had its place,
no longer offers comfort.

I shake off the bells and whistles of
my known existence
in the hopes of
being known again;
being ever re-membered
at every turn to a
restored appearance
while knowing Truth which
always was and always will be.

Blessing Brave Mother Earth with Our Love
by Cathleen Alexander

Blessings come to those who wait and to those who cannot wait.
Some blessings come in despite of problems and some because of
problems, in response to problems.
Spirit has a sense of humor; can we laugh at our mistakes?
Unicorns are unifyingly gifted.
You are God's unique gift to the world, of the world. Our world.

Our Mother Earth is brave to have us here,
let us be brave to give her honor and respect.
Her storms and sunshine are gentle Powers, powerful protection
for her children.
She sends us a white dove of peace to remind us of our unique
experience. This can be a blessing in disguise.

What are your blessings?
Would you prefer a smooth highway or a bumpy dirt road?
Perfection is in the eye of the beholder.
What do you see as your blessings?
Do you rejoice when you're happy?
Do you cry when you are in pain?
I do.

This is a time for blessings, a time for rain;
After the sunshine, a time for pain.
My time is running out. I might be running out. Are you with me?
Can you see me; do I see you?

Our Mother Earth is brave to have us all here.
We love you, dear Mother, some may fear to go against the flow by
stepping out to protect you.
Thank you, dear Planet for providing my path to walk, jump and run
on; to play, skip and dance and play along. We choose our own
paths, different, yet somehow crossing with others.

Let us be brave to give you honor and respect.

Return to Beauty
by Cheryl

What does beauty mean to you?
Is beauty, as they say 'In the eye of the beholder'?
Can we truly judge what is beautiful?

The other day,
a male turkey crossed the road in front of me,
he strutted and sang the whole time.
In effect saying---
Be like me! Strut your stuff! Fan your tail!
Walk like an Egyptian!
Joseph wore a coat of many colors.
We all wear many coats.
He was hated by his brothers
because they deemed him the favorite.

There are no favorites!

We all are---
Shining, Exploding, Becoming,
Returning---

We will not need clothes, cars or passports!
Open UP---
It is time!

Grandmother Tree
Stands
Straight and Tall,
an example
for all of us.

We all are----Beauty.
Shining, Exploding, Becoming,
Returning.

This is a new place
by A'Marie B. Thomas-Brown

Now to unload this burden
of gathered information and
embrace subliminal data,
finding plugs that I was unaware
even existed.

With each new connector, being filled in a posture,
that appeared foreign, now screams familiarity to
the nth degree.

Free to unveil the essence
that has found its
sardonic close to an opening
that serves to remind
until the brilliance blinds
to the power of willed blindness
and deafness.

Free to hear the sound
that is only heard in this state,
of varying dimensions within consciousness,
as to the degree of emptying,
and to remain at rest
amid the traveling salesmen
panning their wares.

I am neither seeking to be sold nor looking to be bought.

I am resolved in the reality, that what was given to the
brilliant death of me, is a perfect picture of revivification.

Grieving and sorrow have their place, as to what they
progress into, is the result of how one saw in the
frame in which they were presented.

As we engage in the face off, the trial commences
with tears streaming down the face of misperception.

Stillness brews within me as I realize our relationship has changed.
This is a new place.

I look Grief in the face
with no curiosity or desire to delve deeper, and
"no further questions, your Honor"
is all I can muster
as we sat on that bench looking,
while another saw.

We part ways and remain true in that place where
we combusted and brilliance filled the blinding
precipice with peace.

I celebrate the loss
and embrace this new normal
by picking up the shards
placing them in a neat pile
and thus watching them disintegrate
into liquid matter, its pre-gaseous state, where the
beauty of its oblivion awaits me.

Mosaic of Light
by Mikasa Tamara Blue Ray

Shattered patterns, like glass on the ground.
Huge collective release.
Bringing much needed peace.
Glass on the ground, a mosaic of light.
Reflecting a future, hopeful and bright. Grace.
New path unfolding, in our collective space.

Le Petit Mort
by Bonnie Bailey

The gentle power
Of imperfectly
Facing your fears.

A brave surrender.

The impinging world-
Tamed.
A gentle child.

Overcoming, though
Afraid.

Consciousness trapped
In time travel.

A spirit sensing home
In the buoyancy
Of self love.

In blessings
Unlimited.

The Universe pulses
In a heartbeat
Of fears
Surrendered.

We Come With Our Hearts White Open
by Rune Darling

From Beyond the Stars
Travelers in Time and Space
.

We bring with Us
The essence of Love
A Cosmic Frequency
.

A Love that will Transform
Everyone Who comes in contact with it
.

Worldly concerns
Problems and sorrows
Dissolving in Our Presence
.

We bring joy and peace to All
We don't bring it as a gift
Since it can't be survived
.

We bring a frequency that you can access
For you already contain everything we bring
.

We are nothing but the vibrational spark
Where do you ignite your DNA
.

You are your own great Alchemist
You can ignite the flames of love
.

On Earth - In heart and soul
In every creature you meet on your path
Once you have lighted your own fire
.

Through your Unconditional Love
Do we merge into existence
.

All opposites unite in Us
We will now light our Soul candle on Earth
.

The Inner
by Janine Savient
The inner fire is real...

Know yourself in freedom
dare to spread your wings
Listen deeply to your heart
hear the song it sings

Feel your courage growing
remember this worlds game
Now, your presence glowing
realize why you came

Lean into your mastery
step forward and be heard
Unleash the inner power,
be integral with every word

Stand solid in your centre
grounded sure and true
You're here for deeper purpose
the knowing is in you

Wear your truth, fully
touch others as you can
Be loves clear example
for every child, woman and man

We're in this change together
in a world tipped upside down
Rise into your power, now
within all, love is found

Know your doubts are leaving
realize love is always the clue
Trust in the inner changes
all fear dissolves now in you

As the world cries out
for blessed purity
Your heart opens,
invested in its surety

Closing Prayer
by Pradeep Nawarathna

May heaven's light shine warm upon your face,
May gentle strength surround you every day.

May wisdom guide each step you choose to take,
And courage lift you when you lose your way.

May joy surprise you in the smallest things,
May peace embrace you when the world grows loud.

May love abundant fill your deepest heart,
And hope remain when darkness forms a cloud.

May all your prayers find answers in good time,
May all your tears be dried by gentle hands.

May faith sustain you through your hardest trials,
And grace support you where you cannot stand.

Many thanks to these contributors:

Ulrikke Aagaard
Cathleen Alexander
Bonnie Bailey
A'Marie B. Thomas-Brown
Elizabeth M. Carillo
Lira Rene Christian
Dan Crusey
Rune Darling
Danielle Divinity
Dave Harvey
Jennifer Hershelman
Jonathan Hopkins
Lilapa
Kazi Ayaz Mahesar
Vivian Marie McIntosh
Shima Moore
Rene Moraida
Pradeep Nawarathna (pcnawarathna@gmail.com)
Mikasa Tamara Blue Ray
Sabina and Herd of Light
Janine Savient
Shivrael
Daniel Stone
Mercy Talley
Archi Thorne
Snow Thorner
'Greenie' Yvonne Trafton
Zarah Chelsie Nicole Wolivar
Le'Vell Zimmerman

Author page--

Cheryl Lunar Wind lives in the Mount Shasta area in a little town called Weed. She is a practicer of Mayan cosmology, Lakota ceremony, Star Knowledge and the Universal Laws including the Law of One. Her hobbies are writing poetry, music, dance, drum circles and love for all life; plant, animal and crystal. Cheryl has been a guide and spiritual teacher for many years. Now she shares wit and wisdom through poetry, and has published poetry books; Know Your Way, We Are One, Follow the White Rabbit, Love Your Light, LIFE: Shared thru Poetry, Come to Mount Shasta: Sacred Path Poetry, We Are Light, Finding Our Way Home, We Are Forever, Handshake With the Divine, Grand Rising: A New Day Has Dawned, Star Messages: Codes to Sing, Dance and Live by, Return to Innocence, Bloom Like Nature: Live the Natural Way, Creativity Brings Peace: Create & Share Your Gifts, May Love Lead, The Eventful Flash: Bringing Solar Waves of Change, The Setting Sun, Crossroads of Change, Step Into New Earth and now Blessings Beyond Belief-- I Am: We Are.

Testimonials---

"Cheryl's poetry is very inspiring--particularly the way she compares life with the forces of nature. There is a special element in her poems that opens my heart and fills my soul with divine possiblities."
Giovanna Taormina, Co-Founder, One Circle Foundation

"Cheryl's poems have helped me to uncover and honor my own hidden memories. The beauty of her spirit is evident in each tender, insightful passage."
Marguerite Lorimer, www.earthalive.com

"A rare collection filled with raw, courageous honesty. Thought provoking words that will stop you in your tracks."
Snow Thorner, ED Open Sky Gallery, Montague, California

"When wisdom, guidance, confirming comfort, ect. arrives to us humans--from beings with the perspective of other realms--it is a divine gift. Especially in the form of what we call poetry, and through a being with no agenda; Cheryl Lunar Wind simply shares what source gives her!"---Dragon Love (Thomas) Budde

"Your poems are like zen koans of wisdom."--Shivrael